The Solar System

by Gregory L. Vogt

Consultant:
Ralph Winrich
Former NASA Aerospace Education Specialist

Bridgestone Books
an imprint of Capstone Press
Mankato, Minnesota

Bridgestone Books are published by Capstone Press
1710 Roe Crest Drive, North Mankato, Minnesota 56003.
www.capstonepub.com

Library of Congress Cataloging-in-Publication Data
Vogt, Gregory.
    The solar system / by Gregory L. Vogt.
    p. cm.—(The galaxy)
    Includes bibliographical references and index.
    Summary: Describes the Sun, planets, and other objects in the solar system.
    ISBN-13: 978-0-7368-1385-3 (hardcover)   ISBN-10: 0-7368-1385-3 (hardcover)
    ISBN-13: 978-0-7368-3459-9 (paperback)   ISBN-10: 0-7368-3459-1 (paperback)
    1. Solar system—Juvenile literature. [1. Solar system.] I. Title. II. Series.
QB501.3 .V64 2003
523.2—dc21   2001008130

Editorial Credits
Tom Adamson, editor; Karen Risch, product planning editor; Timothy Halldin,
    series designer; Patrick Dentinger, book designer and illustrator; Kelly Garvin,
    photo researcher

Photo Credits
Archivo Iconografico, S.A./CORBIS, 6
Bill and Sally Fletcher/TOM STACK & ASSOCIATES, 21 (top)
Courtesy of SOHO/EIT consortium. SOHO is a project of international cooperation
    between ESA and NASA, 8
Dr. R. Albrecht, ESA/ESO Space Telescope European Coordinating Facility; NASA, 20
NASA, 4 (Uranus, Pluto), 12, 13, 18
NASA and the NSSDC, 4 (Venus)
NASA—Goddard Space Flight Center/JHUAPL/NLR, 21 (bottom)
NASA/JPL/Malin Space Science Systems, 14 (bottom)
PhotoDisc, Inc., cover, 1, 4 (Mercury, Earth, Mars, Jupiter, Saturn, Neptune), 14 (top),
    16 (both), 19

Printed in the United States of America in North Mankato, Minnesota.
072012
006816R

Table of Contents

Fast Facts about the Planets 4
The Solar System 5
Early Ideas. 7
The Sun 9
Revolution and Rotation 11
Mercury and Venus 12
Earth and Mars. 15
Jupiter and Saturn 17
Uranus and Neptune. 18
Pluto and Smaller Objects. 20

Hands On: Solar System Model. 22
Words to Know. 23
Read More 23
Useful Addresses 24
Internet Sites 24
Index. 24

Fast Facts about the Planets

	Diameter	Average distance from the Sun	Number of moons
Mercury	3,031 miles (4,878 kilometers)	.5 AU	0
Venus	7,521 miles (12,104 kilometers)	.75 AU	0
Earth	7,927 miles (12,756 kilometers)	1 AU	1
Mars	4,222 miles (6,794 kilometers)	1.5 AU	2
Jupiter	88,736 miles (142,800 kilometers)	5 AU	at least 28
Saturn	74,978 miles (120,660 kilometers)	9.5 AU	at least 30
Uranus	31,765 miles (51,118 kilometers)	19 AU	at least 20
Neptune	30,777 miles (49,528 kilometers)	30 AU	at least 8
Pluto	1,485 miles (2,390 kilometers)	39.5 AU	1

The Solar System

The solar system is our home in space. It includes planets, moons, and other objects that move around the Sun. The planets follow paths called orbits.

The closest planet to the Sun is Mercury. Then come Venus and Earth. Farther out are Mars, Jupiter, Saturn, Uranus, Neptune, and Pluto.

Earth orbits the Sun at an average distance of 93 million miles (150 million kilometers). Pluto orbits at an average distance of 3,673 million miles (5,911 million kilometers).

Except for Mercury and Venus, each planet has smaller bodies called moons that orbit it. There are at least 90 moons in the solar system.

The smallest objects in the solar system are comets and asteroids. Comets are made of ice, rock, and frozen gases. Rock and metal make up asteroids.

AU stands for Astronomical Unit. An AU is the distance between Earth and the Sun. One AU is 93 million miles (150 million kilometers).

Long ago, people had different ideas about the solar system and the stars. Some people thought a dark shell with many holes surrounded Earth. The stars were light shining through the holes. Others thought that Earth rode on the back of a giant elephant. Under each of its feet were large swimming turtles.

People's ideas changed as they began to learn more about the sky. For more than 1,000 years, most people believed Earth was the center of the solar system. They thought Earth stood still while the stars, planets, Sun, and Moon moved around it.

About 450 years ago, astronomer Nicolaus Copernicus concluded that the Sun is the center of the solar system. He said that Earth orbits the Sun. People did not accept Copernicus's ideas at first.

Other astronomers later studied Copernicus's ideas. They used telescopes and other instruments to measure the movements of the planets. They helped prove Copernicus was right.

People once thought that Earth was the center of the solar system. They drew models that showed the Sun, the Moon, and planets traveling around Earth.

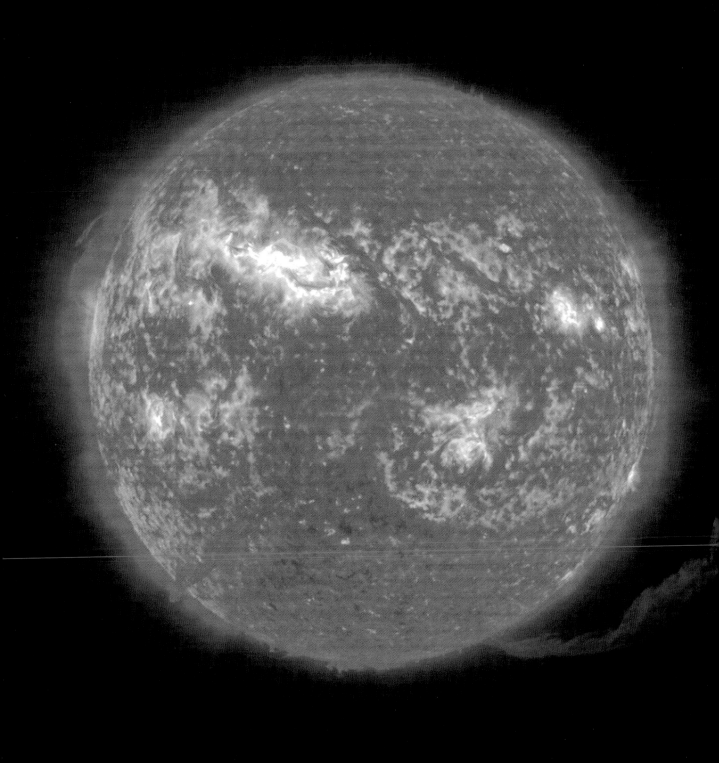

The Sun is a star. Its light and heat reach out to all the planets in the solar system.

The Sun weighs nearly 1,000 times more than the rest of the objects in the solar system combined. The Sun's huge size creates powerful gravity. Gravity keeps the planets moving in orbits around the Sun. Without gravity, the planets would shoot out into deep space.

The Sun is made of the gases hydrogen and helium. Heat and pressure deep inside the Sun turn hydrogen into helium. Some hydrogen turns into light and heat energy. This energy escapes the Sun and warms Earth.

Every second, 4 million tons (3.6 million metric tons) of hydrogen change into energy. This process has been going on for about 5 billion years. The Sun has enough hydrogen to make energy for another 5 billion years.

The Sun is 864,000 miles (1.4 million kilometers) wide.

Relative size of the Sun and the planets

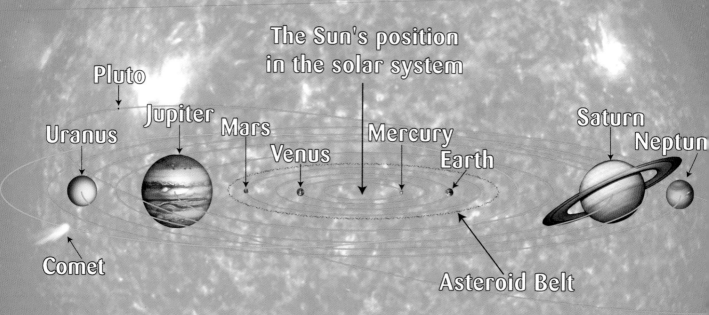

Pluto

Uranus

Jupiter

Mars

Venus

The Sun's position
in the solar system

Mercury

Earth

Saturn

Neptun

Comet

Asteroid Belt

The Sun

The objects in the solar system are in constant motion. Planets revolve around the Sun and moons revolve around planets.

The planets nearest the Sun move the fastest. Mercury orbits the Sun once every 88 days. It zips around the Sun at 30 miles (48 kilometers) per second. Pluto is much farther from the Sun. It travels at a speed of about 3 miles (5 kilometers) per second. Pluto takes 245 Earth years to travel once around the Sun.

The Sun's gravity affects how fast planets orbit. Gravity is stronger the closer the planet is to the Sun. Mercury would fall into the Sun if it traveled any slower than 30 miles per second.

The planets also rotate as they travel around the Sun. Earth rotates once every 24 hours. Jupiter spins around once every 10 hours. Even the Sun rotates. The Sun rotates once every 27 days.

◀ **This illustration compares the sizes of the planets and the Sun. The blue lines show the orbits of the planets. Thousands of asteroids move around the Sun. The asteroid belt is between the orbits of Mars and Jupiter. Chunks of ice and rock called comets also move around the Sun.**

Mercury is the closest planet to the Sun. It is 3,031 miles (4,878 kilometers) wide. Mercury is dark gray and is covered with bowl-shaped holes called craters. The craters were blasted out when Mercury was struck by meteorites, comets, and asteroids.

Mercury has no atmosphere. The side facing the Sun can be up to 800 degrees Fahrenheit (427 degrees Celsius). The side away from the Sun cools off to minus 300 degrees Fahrenheit (minus 184 degrees Celsius).

Craters cover Mercury's surface.

The surface of Venus is hotter than the surface of Mercury.

Venus is the second planet from the Sun. Venus is nearly the same size as Earth and it is covered with thick clouds. Space probes have discovered that Venus has hundreds of large volcanoes. The surface also has many cracks and hundreds of craters.

Although Mercury is closer to the Sun, Venus is hotter. Venus's thick atmosphere captures and holds the Sun's heat. The temperature of Venus is about 900 degrees Fahrenheit (482 degrees Celsius).

Earth is the only planet in the solar system that has large amounts of liquid water.

A long canyon stretches from left to right near the bottom of this photo of Mars.

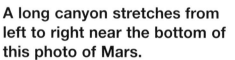

Earth is the third planet from the Sun. Water covers three-fourths of its surface. Earth is 93 million miles (150 million kilometers) away from the Sun. If Earth were closer to the Sun, its oceans would boil away. If it were farther away, the oceans would freeze.

Earth has large continents of dry land. There are mountains, plains, glaciers, and valleys. Earth is home to millions of plants and animals. Plants take in minerals and water from the soil and energy from the Sun. Plants create food for animals. Earth has one large moon.

Mars is about 142 million miles (228 million kilometers) away from the Sun. This small, rocky planet is about half the size of Earth. Mars is a frozen desert and has very little air surrounding it.

Mars has several giant volcanoes. One is more than three times higher than Mount Everest on Earth. One canyon on Mars is longer than the width of the United States. Mars has two small moons.

Jupiter is the largest planet in the solar system. The large storm is called the Great Red Spot. People have observed it for the past 400 years.

People can see Saturn's rings from Earth through a telescope.

The first four planets in the solar system are rocky worlds. Jupiter and Saturn are giant planets made of gases. Jupiter is bigger than the other eight planets combined.

Thick clouds surround Jupiter. The cloud tops form white and orange stripes. These bands and zones surround Jupiter. Swirling storms form at the edges of the bands and zones. One storm has lasted at least 400 years and is twice as large as Earth. This storm is called the Great Red Spot.

Jupiter has one faint ring and at least 28 moons. Four of its moons are larger than Pluto.

Saturn also is a giant gas planet. Thick clouds also surround Saturn. A wide system of thousands of narrow rings circle the planet. The rings are made of dust and pieces of ice and rock. From Earth, Saturn's rings look like a disk.

Saturn has at least 30 moons. One moon has its own thick atmosphere.

The next two planets also are gas giants. Uranus and Neptune are about one-third the size of Jupiter. Uranus is blue-green and is covered with thick clouds. It is a sideways planet. All the other planets travel in their orbits like spinning tops. Uranus lies on its side. It orbits like a rolling ball.

For half of Uranus's orbit, its north pole points toward the Sun. For the other half, the south pole points toward the Sun. Uranus orbits the Sun once every 84 years. Uranus has 11 faint rings and at least 20 moons.

Uranus is blue-green and is covered with thick clouds.

White clouds sometimes appear in Neptune's atmosphere.

The last giant planet is Neptune. Neptune has five faint rings and at least eight moons. Bands of dark clouds circle the planet. Swirling storms of dark or white clouds sometimes appear. Winds drive the cloud bands and the storms around the planet at speeds of 1,240 miles (1,995 kilometers) per hour.

The last planet in the solar system is Pluto. It is 40 times farther from the Sun than Earth is. Pluto is a tiny ice and rock world only 1,485 miles (2,390 kilometers) across. Not much is known about Pluto. It has one moon called Charon. Charon is about half the size of Pluto.

Some people think Pluto should not be called a planet. They think it is a giant comet or asteroid. For now, Pluto is still called a planet.

Astronomers cannot get clear photos of Pluto and Charon because they are so far away from Earth.

Comets are chunks of rock, ice, and gas that orbit the Sun. Comets sometimes get very close to the Sun and start melting. They release gas and dust. The gas and dust stretch out to form a long tail.

Asteroids are large chunks of space rock and metal. Some asteroids are hundreds of miles or kilometers across while others are a few yards or meters across. Most asteroids travel in broad orbits between Mars and Jupiter.

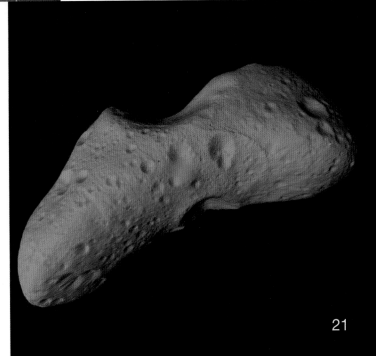

Hands On: Solar System Model ☾

See how far apart planets are from each other by making a model of the solar system.

What You Need

Sidewalk
Sidewalk chalk
Ruler or tape measure

What You Do

1. Draw a small circle on the sidewalk and write the word "Sun" next to it.
2. Using a ruler or tape measure, measure 5 inches (13 centimeters) from the Sun. Draw a small dot and mark it as Mercury.
3. In the same direction, measure 9 inches (23 centimeters) from the Sun and make a dot for Venus.
4. Mark dots for the rest of the planets in the solar system according to the chart above.

Planet	Distance from Sun in Model
Mercury	5 inches (13 centimeters)
Venus	9 inches (23 centimeters)
Earth	12 inches (30 centimeters)
Mars	18 inches (46 centimeters)
Jupiter	5 feet, 3 inches (1.6 meters)
Saturn	9 feet, 7 inches (2.9 meters)
Uranus	19 feet, 3 inches (5.9 meters)
Neptune	30 feet, 1 inch (9.2 meters)
Pluto	39 feet, 5 inches (12 meters)

The model you made shows the planets stretched out in a straight line. Normally, the planets are spread out around the Sun. The model you made shows the distance between each orbit. In a model this size, the Sun would only be about the size of a grain of sand. Earth would be too tiny to be visible without a microscope.

Words to Know

atmosphere (AT-muhss-feehr)—the mixture of gases that surrounds some planets and moons

gravity (GRAV-uh-tee)—a force that pulls objects together

meteorite (MEE-tee-ur-rite)—a piece of space rock that strikes a planet or a moon

orbit (OR-bit)—the path of an object as it moves around another object in space

revolution (rev-uh-LOO-shuhn)—the movement of one object around another object in space

rotation (roh-TAY-shuhn)—one complete spin of an object in space

telescope (TEL-uh-skope)—an instrument that makes faraway objects appear larger and closer

Read More

Cooper, Christopher. *Solar System*. Science Fact Files. Austin, Texas: Raintree Steck-Vaughn, 2001.

Davis, Kenneth C. *Don't Know Much about the Solar System*. New York: HarperCollins, 2001.

Gallant, Roy A. *Comets, Asteroids, and Meteorites*. Kaleidoscope. Tarrytown, N.Y.: Benchmark Books, 2001.

Vogt, Gregory. *Solar System*. Scholastic Science Readers. New York: Scholastic Reference, 2001.

Useful Addresses

Lowell Observatory
1400 West Mars Hill Road
Flagstaff, AZ 86001

The Planetary Society
65 North Catalina Avenue
Pasadena, CA 91106-2301

NASA Headquarters
Washington, DC 20546-0001

Internet Sites

FactHound offers a safe, fun way to find Internet sites related to this book. All of the sites on FactHound have been researched by our staff.

Here's all you do:
Visit *www. facthound.com*
Type in this code: 0736813853
FactHound will fetch the best sites for you!

Index

asteroid, 5, 11, 12, 20, 21
atmosphere, 12, 13, 17, 19
comet, 5, 11, 12, 20, 21
craters, 12, 13
Earth, 4, 5, 7, 9, 11, 13, 14, 15, 16, 17, 20
gravity, 9, 11
Jupiter, 4, 5, 11, 16, 17, 18, 21
Mars, 4, 5, 11, 14, 15, 21

Mercury, 4, 5, 11, 12, 13
moon, 4, 5, 7, 11, 15, 17, 18, 19, 20
Neptune, 4, 5, 18, 19
Pluto, 4, 5, 11, 17, 20
rings, 16, 17, 18, 19
Saturn, 4, 5, 16, 17
Uranus, 4, 5, 18
Venus, 4, 5, 13